An Amish Christmas Carol
An Amish Christian "Classic"

By
Sarah Price

2012

The Pennsylvania Dutch used in this manuscript is taken from the
Pennsylvania Dutch Revised Dictionary (1991) by C. Richard Beam,
Brookshire Publications, Inc. in Lancaster, PA.

Contact the author on Facebook at
http://www.facebook.com/fansofsarahprice or
visit her Web Blog at http://sarahpriceauthor.wordpress.com.

Other Books by Sarah Price

The Amish of Lancaster Series
#1: Fields of Corn
#2: Hills of Wheat
#3: Pastures of Faith
#4: Valley of Hope

The Amish of Ephrata Series
#1: The Tomato Patch
#2: The Quilting Bee
#3: The Hope Chest (2013)
#4: The Clothes Line (2013)

The Amish of Lititz
Plain Fame
Plain Change (2013)
Plain Again (2013)

Amish Circle Letters
Miriam's Letter: Volume 1
Rachel's Letter: Volume 2
Leah's Letter: Volume 3
Anna's Letter: Volume 4
Lizzie's Letter: Volume 5

Sylvia's Letter: Volume 6
Lovina's Letter: Volume 7
Ella's Letter: Volume 8
Mary Ruth's Letter: Volume 9
Miriam's Package: Volume 10

The Adventures of a Family Dog Series
#1: A Small Dog Named Peek-a-boo
#2: Peek-a-boo Runs Away
#3: Peek-a-boo's New Friends
#4: Peek-a-boo and Daisy Doodle

Other Books
Gypsy in Black
Postcards from Abby (with Ella Stewart)
Meet Me in Heaven (with Ella Stewart)
Mark Miller's One Volume 11: The Power of Faith
A Gift of Faith: An Amish Christmas Story
A Christmas Gift for Rebecca: An Amish Christian Romance
Fields of Zombies: An Amish Parable (with Sam Lang)

Dedication

For those of us who have lost a loved one recently, the holiday seasons can be especially tough. We find ourselves left behind with an empty spot in our heart. We live through memories of happier days, filled with love and laughter that we shared with those who have passed before us. But, no matter whom you miss or how heavy that ache in your heart may be, just know that *you are not alone.* Even those who feel that there is not one person left to care for them must remember that there is, indeed, one who cares greatly for us and loves us: God.

Table of Contents

A Word from the Author

First of all, since you are reading this letter, I have to presume that you have purchased...or at least borrowed...this book. For that, I want to thank you.

That brings me to my next point. Perhaps you may have noticed that there are a lot of books being published in the Amish Christian genre. I'm amazed at how many aspiring and talented authors have started publishing their books about the Amish. When I first published Fields of Corn in 2009, there were just a handful of authors on Amazon.com. Today, there are dozens!

With that being said, I took a good look at the other books that are out there as well as my own books. I decided to try something new and different. You see, I am an author, a dedicated writer who has a passion for the written word and is often consumed with obsession over the act of writing. Being an author is not one bit different than any other profession.

I've decided to raise the literary bar on my writing...and on your reading. This book is the first of what I hope will be many books that follow that retell literary classics from the perspective of the Amish. This will allow both you and I to refresh our memories about the classics while sharing the Amish culture and Amish religion.

I'm hoping that this journey takes both of us to a new level, a new place that transcends a simple romance and becomes...well...an Amish classic. You will recognize similarities but you will also recognize difference in this retelling of Charles Dickens' A Christmas Carol. I'm confident that the twist on this tale will warm your heart, keep you entertained, and satisfied your desire to learn more about the world of the Amish.

After twenty-five years of studying and living among the Amish and having been raised Mennonite, I consider myself a good source of information about these amazing people. Their culture and their religion fascinate me. I must confess that writing these stories is not really work...it's a joy, a true blessing, that I am able to share, with my readers, all of my experiences with, knowledge of, and passion for the Amish.

Indeed, I have been blessed with a successful writing career and I cannot tell you how many mornings I wake up to lovely emails or messages on Facebook from my readers that just warm my heart. Sometimes I have to pinch myself for, truly, from the very earliest age, all I ever wanted to do was write.

You have made that possible.

So thank you for purchasing (or borrowing) this book. Thank you for reading it. And thank you for being as enthralled with the Amish as I am.

With blessings and wishing for a wonderful holiday season, this year and every year!

Hugs,

Sarah Price

Chapter One

It was Christmas Eve and Elsie sat in her rocking chair, bent over the afghan that she was crocheting. She rocked back and forth, the chair creaking against the worn wooden floor. With her foot, she tried to move the hand-woven rag rug that was under the chair so that the floor wouldn't make such a racket. It didn't work. Unless she stood up to move the chair, she couldn't do it. Ignoring the noise, she continued to focus on the afghan.

While her finger moved so quickly that anyone who tried to watch it would be want to figure out how she did it. The afghan was a series of blues: dark blue, sky blue, light blue, and pale blue. Blue was her favorite color, after all. The colors alternated with each row, neat shell-stitches that fanned out like seashell on the beach. She was currently working on the pale blue row, which was easier on her 75 year old, eyes, especially since the sun was starting to dip behind the fields outside of her front window.

The clock chimed. One. Two. Three. Four. Each chime reverberated in the empty room and she lowered her hands to glance at it as if in disbelief that it was already four o'clock. She took a deep breath and let her head fall back onto the chair's headrest. In just a few short hours, it would be Christmas, a day that, in the past, brought her great joy. However, this year, she was dreading the next 24 hours.

Her aging blue eyes traveled to the window. There were no curtains on the window so that she would always have sunlight in the room. Now, however, the sun was setting. Elsie watched the sky turn from orange to a deep red and the sun

continued to set. She watched it for a g[...]
mind wandering to the past holidays w[...]
she felt happier.

Was it only seven weeks ag[...]
passed away? The last of her sibling, [...]
seemed as if it was only yesterday that he had p[...]
hoped it would get easier with each passing day but, since she
had never married, she had no more immediate family, and her
days were spent alone for the most part.

Stephen had been ill for a while but Elsie had taken care
of him for several years. After all, she had told everyone in her
church district, that was what family was for. So she had
changed his bed, wiped his face, and cleaned his clothes while
he had diminished as a person over the years.

The signs had been subtle at first. He couldn't
remember who hosted the Sunday church service the week
before last. Then he was questioning who was the bishop of
their district, demanding that Elsie was telling him wrong
when she said it was Jacob Beiler. Finally, the day arrived when
he questioned Elsie about who she was and where was his
mother, for she alone was the sole caretaker of him, he argued.

"Nee, Stephen," Elsie had soothed, wiping the
applesauce from his face with a clean, blue and white napkin.
"Mamm has been dead for ten years, bruder. It is your sister,
Elsie, who tends your needs now."

He had waved her hand away from the hospital bed that
was set up in the living room before the large picture window.
Elsie had chosen to set up his sickbed in that room because it
was bright and cheerful with a greyish blue paint on the walls
and plants in the fall when she brought them inside from the

. Stephen also loved to watch the birds at the bird
ach morning and afternoon. The light of the day didn't
r him at all, he claimed.

"I know you not!" he had shouted.

Elsie had felt despair over his words. How could her
bruder, the only remaining sibling of ten, not remember her?
She was, after all, Elsie Smucker, the sister who had tended to
all of their needs in their final hours. Sister Lizzie had died
from a stroke but it was Elsie who wiped her brow with a cool
cloth before she passed to join Jesus in the after life. Sister
Anna had died in her home, softly asleep with a mild purr that,
for some odd reason, had awakened Elsie from her bedroom
next door. As for the other siblings, they had passed away on
their on...two by their own hand which was something that
wasn't talked about among the family and three by sickness in
their early adult years.

There had been ten of them, growing up together and
laughing away the casual years of their youth. No one had
given much thought to the future, that was for sure and certain.
And when Elsie was thirty years old, she had looked around
with wide and surprised eyes, shocked to realize that all of her
friends had married already and were on their third or fourth
baby. What had she done during those formative years while
they were starting a family?

Nothing.

"Oh help," she whispered and shut her eyes at the
repeat memory of her past. Yes, she thought, I did nothing but
what a life I have lived.

Her eyelids felt heavy as she thought back to years past.
There were so many memories of winters past, of fast paced

rides in horse drawn sleighs, of turns in homemade saucers that flew down the hills with lightening speed into the frozen stream, and snowball fights in the back fields of their parents' farm, far enough from the house so that their mamm and daed wouldn't see the pseudo-war that took place without the perimeter of their peaceful home.

She didn't know when things had changed, that was for sure and certain. For so many years, she had been just having fun, laughing with friends and enjoying life. Slowly, one by one, those friends had married off during the wedding season, November and December of each year. She had enjoyed those weddings, loving the happiness that exuded from her friend's expressions as they stared at their beloved. But she, Elsie Smucker, had never found that love or happiness, not in her youth, that was for sure and certain.

And then, one day, she realized that she was the last of her friends who had been married. Her friends were beginning to have swollen bellies from the babies growing within them. Elsie made as much as a fuss as she could over her friends but, without having experienced a life growing within her own body, she was at a loss. She could only imagine what they felt and that, by itself, was a hard stretch of her imagination.

Indeed, by the time she had turned thirty, her chances to marry as a young woman were over. The speculation began to surface that a widower would marry Elsie Smucker. That was a thought that she didn't cherish one bit. She was happier alone and didn't need a husband to complete her. Of that, she was sure and certain.

It wasn't as if she hadn't dated. No, that wasn't the case. She just hadn't fancied any of the young men who did come calling. As for the men that she had considered suitable, well...they didn't seem to fancy her one bit. Elsie reckoned it was fair and never complained. Instead, she continued to work at the market, selling her daed's vegetables and meats alongside her mamm's homemade cheese. On her off days, she helped tend her sisters' children or, for a few years, cleaned a neighbor's house on Mondays. As the years passed, she continued to live with her parents in the farmhouse, wishing with all of her might that life might have granted her a different journey. Yet, as soon as she thought it, she prayed forgiveness for she knew that the Lord had chosen this path for her. Who was she to question it?

Her daed was almost 70 years old when he sold the farm to bruder Isaac so that he could raise his family and become a proper farmer. As the baby of the family, Isaac had only been a young man and his family just beginning. Daed was too old to work the mules in the field and muck stalls each day. So he purchased the small ranch house off Route 340 outside of Gordonville for living out his final years with his wife and sole dochder who still resided at home: Elsie.

That had been over 25 years ago.

Daed passed away at 80. Mamm followed five years later. She had only been 78 when she joined their daed in heaven. And that left Elsie alone in the house to continue taking care of her siblings and their families that were left behind when they passed.

Now, at 75 years of age, Elsie Smucker was alone. Her world revolved around her meals, her crocheting, and her devotionals. She read them incessantly, wearing down the pages to the point that the edges were blurred from her fingers holding the book open. She read the Ausbund, too. She could read the words of each hymn and, without shutting her eyes, fall down a time warp to the past, hearing the voices since the songs during church service or gatherings. After all, 75 years was a long time to have listened to those hymns.

She heard the familiar noise of an approaching horse and buggy pulling down the road. The horse's shoes clip-clopped against the pavement and the gentle rattle of the buggy wheels followed. Her eyes traveled back to the window, wondering who was traveling at 4:30 on Christmas Eve. As the buggy passed, she could see two children hanging out the back window. They waved at her as they passed.

She smiled.

Long after the noise had faded, she still sat in her chair. She had always hoped that she'd have children. When she was younger, she had thought she'd get married young and have at least eight or more children before she was mid-thirty.

Some dreams weren't meant to come true.

But she took comfort in the fact that she had loved her family, tending to their care as they aged and were too sick to stay at home. Most importantly, she had been by their sides during their final hours. Some of them, anyway. Yet, she had the nagging question that haunted her each night: *Who will take care of me?*

It didn't matter, she supposed. Not now. She had lived her life according to the Lord's plan and she couldn't second-guess the choices she had made. Perhaps she'd have to move to the home on the hill with the other Amish and Mennonites who were too sick to be at home with their families or didn't have families to take care of them. Elsie looked around the house that had been her home for so long. While she didn't mind not dying here, she told herself, she certainly didn't want to die *there.* Cold rooms. Sterile smells. Strange noises. Strangers. No, she much preferred to die alone...in this house if the Lord saw fit...and hopefully without suffering.

"Best get some tea before starting supper," she said out loud to no one.

She shuffled into the kitchen and reached for the kettle to put onto the stove. It was empty. She could feel that by how light it felt when she lifted it.

"Oh bother," she mumbled and returned over to the sink. She flipped the handle and let the water run for a few seconds before she began to fill it. The room was darker now that the sun had set and she knew she'd have to light the kerosene lanterns soon. But she wasn't in a hurry. They threw off such a loud hiss followed by heat that she wanted to wait before lighting them.

Her eyes travelled to the window. Outside was a small bird feeder hanging from a metal bracket that her daed had hung so many years ago. Each spring, she painted it black with Rust-o-leum in order to keep it from rusting away. The bird feeder was empty. She frowned. Hadn't she just filled it that morning?

She shut off the water and started to turn back to the stove when a shadow passed by the window. It was a subtle movement but enough to catch her eye. She stopped in her tracks and turned to look outside. Nothing. She set the kettle on the counter and rubbed at her eyes beneath her glasses. What could have made that shadow, she wondered. *Am I seeing things?*

Dropping her hands from her eyes, she squinted and looked one more time. There. By the birdfeeder. She could barely make out something that looked so familiar yet so strange. Elsie leaned against the counter and moved closer to the window. There it was indeed. A face. No body, just a face. Almost like a vapor lingering by the birdfeeder.

I'm seeing things, she told herself, quickly backing away. *I must be getting dementia!*

Once again, she rubbed her eyes and looked out the window, scolding herself for giving herself such a fright. Certainly she hadn't seen a face in the birdfeeder. It simply could not be, she told herself. This time, the birdfeeder was just that: a birdfeeder. No face. No vapor. No Stephen.

"I best be sitting down," she whispered. Forgetting about her tea or preparing her supper, she hurried back into the sitting room and quickly drew the curtains shut around the windows. Then, in the darkness, she sat down in her chair. She clasped her arms around herself, rocking back and forth as she tried to make sense of what she thought she had just seen.

But it didn't make sense.

Everyone knew that once someone died, their earthly body went into the ground while their spiritual body lifted to the heavens. At least, if they were a godly person. Stephen had certainly been that. He had always been the first person willing to help others. He assisted the elderly, helped those with financial struggles, and went out of his way to support those in emotional need. He was in heaven, Elsie told herself. Not in my backyard.

A few minutes passed and she was beginning to calm down. *My nerves,* she thought. *It's just my nerves, still raw from his death and on edge about my first Christmas alone.* Truth was that she missed her bruder. They had a special relationship, especially since they were so close in age. He was much more than just a bruder. He was also her friend. A piece of her had died with him.

It was growing darker out and Elsie felt a wave of sorrow wash over herself. She shut her eyes, trying to push the sadness from her heart. Her rocking slowed and she began to feel herself drifting away. *A small nap*, she told herself. That's all she needed. Just half an hour and then should be make supper. Nothing fancy. Mayhaps just a sandwich and reheated soup.

Her breathing slowed down and her head dipped to the side. And the sky continued to grow darker outside the windows in the sitting room.

Chapter Two

She awoke with a start. The clock had just chimed five times. For a moment, she tried to understand why she had awoken. The final chime of the clock was still reverberating. Yet, she knew that it wasn't the noise of the elegant timepiece on the bookcase that had startled her from her nap. It was a feeling. A feeling that she wasn't alone in the house. It was dark in the room and she reached on the table by her chair for the flashlight. She regretted now that she hadn't turned on the kerosene lantern in the kitchen earlier. The glow from that would reach into the sitting room.

"Hello?" she called out, forcing herself to stand and slowly approach the doorway into the kitchen. "Who's there?"

No answer.

Her heart pounded inside of her chest and, for the briefest of moments, she wondered if she was either dreaming or dying. Certainly it was one of the two, she thought. There was no noise in the house, not even the ticking from the clock that had just chimed. The air felt thick and heavy, a gentle pressure around herself.

"Elsie," a voice said softly behind her.

She spun around and almost dropped the flashlight.

"Elsie," the voice repeated. "Be not afraid."

Surprisingly, with the words, her fear vanished. Instead, she felt a calmness wash over her. Furthermore, with the sense of calmness that she experiences, another sensation followed: happiness. For the first time in such a while, she felt happy. And by feeling happy, she knew that she hadn't been for a very long time.

"Stephen?" she asked, her voice sounding far too normal and at ease with talking to someone who had passed away seven weeks ago. "Are you there?"

"Come walk with me," the voice said.

Elsie wasn't certain what was happening. Surely she was dreaming. *Or dying,* she thought. Was this how her life was to end? On Christmas Eve and alone with a voice that sounded strangely like her beloved brother, Stephen?

Still, as before, she was at peace and, without knowing how or why, she found herself standing beside the vaporous image of her brother at the family farm from years ago. It wasn't winter anymore but summertime. Elsie smiled as she stared at the image of her mamm hanging the laundry on the line while the kinner ran about the yard in the late morning sun.

"It's Mamm!" Elsie whispered.

"Keep looking," said the gentle voice of her bruder.

The black and white Holstein cows wandered through the back meadow. Beyond that, the growing crop of sweet corn blessed the horizon. A gentle breeze caused the green stalks to sway, just a little, and it created a musical melody that was oh so familiar.

In the distance, Elsie could make out the faint image of a man. He was working the team of mules as they pulled a cutter along the field of growing hay. His battered straw hat was pushed back on his head as he turned to say something to someone on the other side of the cutter.

Within seconds, Elsie saw her two older brothers run to catch up with him. She caught her breath and clapped her

18

hands in delight. It had been years since Jonah and John David had taken their own lives, both struggling with illnesses that had deteriorated their quality of life. Such sorrow and shame their deaths had brought to the community and family. Yet, Elsie had understood that they had made the decision after much consideration. It would be too expensive to spend the remainder of their lives under medical care in a facility and their families would be hard pressed to tend to their needs. Both had gone quietly in the night, their own choice and at their own time. No one had ever spoken about it again.

"Daed and the boys!" she whispered, fighting the urge to cry.

She missed her daed. He had been a right gut man with a quick smile and twinkling eyes that were always bright and cheerful. He laughed a lot, even at the small things such as a kitten playing with a leaf in the yard or a naughty mule that broke through the fencing of its paddock. His gut sense of humor had been contagious, a trait that made him a very well-liked member of the community.

When he had passed, Elsie had been holding his hand. She had felt the peace descend from above and cover his body as his spirit lifted. Without anyone telling her, she knew that he was gone. For a long moment, she had sat by his side, the warmth of his hand slowly ebbing from hers. She just wanted to remember him for a moment without interference from her mamm or the bishop or siblings. He had been a special part of Elsie's life and she had would miss him, despite knowing that he now walked with the Lord and Jesus.

Her thoughts were interrupted as Stephen prodded her with a simple, "And whom else do you see?"

"Why, I don't know," Elsie responded. Wasn't it enough that she had just seen her mamm, daed, and bruders? The warm memories filled her with a joy that she knew she would treasure forever. She couldn't imagine why she was having this dream but she knew that it was quite special, indeed. The Lord had seen fit to give her this dream on Christmas Eve and what a magical present that was!

However, at Stephen's urging, she squinted and looked as hard as she could, trying to find the answer that Stephen sought.

It only took a minute. There was a movement away from the house. Indeed, once she saw that flash of dark green, she spotted it easily: a young girl standing alone by the side of the barn, comforting an even smaller boy. The girl wore a dark green dress with a black apron and a white handkerchief was tied over her head. During chore time, she was less inclined to wear her prayer kapp so that she didn't have to bleach it for Sunday service. Her feet were bare and dirty as only Amish children can have and still make parents' smile.

She was leaning over the little boy who wore a blue shirt and black pants with suspenders. His straw hat was on the ground beside him. One of his pant legs was rolled up and he was crying as the little girl inspected a large wound on his leg.

"Why, that's me!" Elsie gasped. Had she ever been that young, she wondered. This time, the tears came to her eyes and she brushed them aside as she watched. Her dark hair was pulled back and she was so thin. Her waist had not yet thickened with age, following years of pecan pies, homemade bread and mashed potatoes.

"And me," said Stephen gently pointed out. "I remember this day so vividly, Sister Elsie. You stopped playing when the others wouldn't, just to tend to my injury. You even carried me from the side of the barn to Mamm so that I wouldn't have to put pressure on my leg." He paused. "I never forgot that moment nor the many other sacrifices that you made during your life. You always seemed to be tending to others, especially me, and missing the brighter moments in life."

Elsie watched as the little girl scooped the boy into her arms and, just as Stephen had said, carried her over the driveway and the yard to the house so that Mamm could tend to his wound. She had forgotten about that day and, even now as she watched her memory replay it, she had a hard time placing exactly when that happened. As Stephen had pointed out, it was just one of many incidents in her lifetime where she had stopped whatever she was doing to tend the needs of others.

"I have come to visit you, Elsie," Stephen said, his voice smooth and pleasant. "You need to be reminded of the good that you have done in your life, the sacrifices that you have made on behalf of others. A decision will come your way and I know that you will have a struggle with it. But I also know that you will choose the right way."

Elsie forced herself to turn her eyes away from the mesmerizing scene that was unfolding on the porch before her. She longed to keep watching, to see her sweet Mamm tend to young Stephen's wounds, wiping away the blood and rewarding his tears with a homemade cookie. But the words that Stephen had just spoken confused her.

"A decision?" she asked, her voice high pitched and incredulous. "Why, what kind of decision would I possibly have?" She almost laughed at the thought. These days, her decisions were focused on what to eat for meals, the colors to crochet her afghans, or what time to walk to the mailbox for the day's correspondence.

"A life changing decision," he said.

Life changing? At 75 years of age? She laughed out loud. Truly, she couldn't help herself. "Stephen," she began. "I'm at the end of my life. I can feel that I only have a few years left. There are no decisions left that could change my life at this point." After all, she thought to herself, there is no one left to help except herself.

"You will see," he said, his voice barely a whispered. "Just remember, when it comes, that this vision is more than just a dream."

She gasped. How had he known that she thought it was a dream?

"Yes, Elsie," he soothed. "I know what you are thinking. And this is not a dream but a gift, a gift to a woman who spent her life putting others first." He paused. "Now it is your time."

"I don't understand," she whispered, turning to look at Stephen. But he was gone. She turned back to look at the farm and that, too, was gone. Everything was dark and black, blacker than the dead of night. She felt nothing, saw nothing, smelled nothing. She was alone once again and her head felt a bit fuzzy.

Had she really just visited with her bruder? Or was she, too, experiencing the onset of dementia?

Chapter Three

The sharp knock at the kitchen door startled her from her sleep. She looked around the dark sitting room, relieved to know that she had, indeed, been dreaming. Stephen had not visited her and spoken to her. The dream had seemed so real that the feeling of peace and happiness was still swelling inside of her chest. He had seemed so...there.

There was another knock at the door. The glass rattled and she could see that the sensor light was on, eliminated the front porch.

Elsie reached for her flashlight and clicked it on as she stood up and made her way to the kitchen. Her battery-operated motion sensor outside of the door was one, illuminating the front porch. She could see the outline of a man, his back to the door, through the glass. From the black hat upon his head and the dark suit, she could tell right away that it was an Amish man.

She unlocked the door and opened it, peering outside to see who had come visiting on Christmas Eve.

"Elsie," the man said. "How are you this evening?"

"Why Bishop Beiler!" She took a step back, smiling at her old friend. "Come in, come in!"

"It's just Jacob, Elsie. We go back far too long to be anything other than Jacob and Elsie," he said gently.

She felt her heart catch in her throat. At one point in time, she had hoped to be Jacob's Elsie. Her bitterness over his marriage to Mary King had faded many decades ago. But she still thought back to that one question that haunted her: *What if?*

"What brings you here, Bis...Jacob?" she asked.

He glanced around the kitchen and frowned. "It's so dark in here, Elsie. Let me light the lantern, ja?" He didn't wait for her answer as he hurried to the table where the kerosene lantern hung. He looked around for a moment until he spied the black metal box on the wall where she kept her matches. Within a few seconds, he had struck the match against the strike plate and lit the lantern. The hiss was first and then the warm glow that filled the room.

With a quick movement, he shook out the match and turned to look for the garbage. It was by the kitchen sink. As he tossed it inside the bin, he noticed the water bubbling on the stove. "Were you expecting someone, then?" he asked, glancing at the kettle.

"Nee, nee," she gushed. "Not at all. I was making myself some tea. Chamomile tea." She hurried over to the cabinet to pull out a mug and her tea bags. "It helps me sleep, you know. Would you care for some?"

"Ja," he said. "Sounds right gut. Don't mind if I do."

Elsie gestured toward the table. "Have a seat, Jacob. Won't take me but a minute," she said as she hustled to set up the mugs and the tea bags before pouring the water over them. She was quiet while she worked, anxious to make the tea just right...not too weak and certainly not too bitter.

"Saw your house was dark as I was passing," Jacob explained as he reached up to take off his hat. He placed it on the bench next to where he sat. "Wanted to check on you, seeing that you are alone this Christmas."

"That was right kind of you," she said in response, trying

to ignore the way her stomach dropped at the reminder that she was alone for the holiday.

"Saw your nephew Menno here the other day, no?"

Carefully, so that she wouldn't spill any of the tea (for then she'd have to wash the floor and working on Christmas was not something she wanted to do), she carried the two mugs to the table then returned to the kitchen area for the milk, sugar, and two spoons. "Oh ja, he came by to put my storm windows in," she replied. Setting the two mugs of coffee on the table, she finally sat down to join the bishop, curious as to why he was visiting her, indeed. "He's a right gut man, that Menno."

"Danke," he said as he took the mug. "That he is. Seems to be over here often to tend to things around your house." Jacob reached for the pretty china sugar bowl and lifted the lid. "Was this your mamm's?" he asked as he dipped his spoon into it for a generous helping of sweetener.

"Ja, it was," she asked. "She left me the china when she passed but requested I pass it along to one of my nieces or nephews when I die."

He raised an eyebrow but said nothing. It wasn't uncommon for gifts to be bequeathed to others with a request for its next owner afterwards. Quite often, items were found in cupboards or shelves with a piece of paper inside or underneath, usually a yellowed piece of paper, with a name scribbled on it. That was the only will that Amish had for the little things.

"How's his boy?"

Elsie looked up, surprised by the question. "You mean Timothy?"

"Ja," the bishop said, nodding his head. "Haven't seen the boy since the accident last year."

Elsie stared into her cup and tried not to think of the accident with the hay cutter. Had it really been almost eighteen months since small Timothy, only seven at the time, had run in front of the mules, spooking them and getting trampled? It was his left foot that had gotten cut up so badly that the doctors had to amputate it just above the ankle. "They are making due," Elsie said simply. "Melinda sure is gut with that boy," she added. "They all are."

The bishop nodded.

Farming accidents happened too frequently in their community. Children got kicked by horses, farmers got injured in the fields, barns burned down due to smoldering hay that was baled too quickly and weren't dried properly. Sometimes the outcome was worse than losing a limb. Sometimes lives were lost. It was a tragic reality in Lancaster County, Pennsylvania, but it never got any easier to accept.

"How you getting on, Elsie?" he asked, setting the spoon on the table and lifting the mug to his lips. He blew once on the liquid, squinting as the hot steam created a fog on his glasses.

"Getting on?" she repeated but she knew what he meant. It was a question that many people asked her. It was the preferred way to address an uncomfortable situation, she often thought. People didn't know what to say to her. They felt awkward knowing that she was a maedel, living alone and with no more immediate family to help tend her needs. The awkwardness of that situation left people with only one question: to inquire how she was *getting on.*

"Why, I'm right gut, I reckon," Elsie answered truthfully.

"As gut as one can be at my age," she added.

"Your age is my age, not?"

She laughed. "Oh ja, we sure do go back many years, don't we, Bis...Jacob," she corrected herself.

He took a short sip of the tea then set the mug down. "Do you remember that teacher we had when we were..." He glanced to the floor, trying to remember. "Thirteen, I reckon, ja? Well, at least I was. You would have been a bit younger, not? It was that teacher that came from Ohio."

Elsie frowned. Ohio? She couldn't remember a teacher from...A smile broke on to her face. "Oh ja! That Linda Zook! Why, I had forgotten all about that woman! She sure had it in for you, didn't she, now?"

Jacob laughed, the corners of his eyes crinkling with deep wrinkles. "That she did! But I seem to remember that you could do no wrong her eyes. The best in spelling, the best in geometry, the best in English." The way he said it told her that he bore her no grudge. Instead, there was a hint of pride in his voice. "You were a right gut student," he said softly.

With a simple wave of her hand, Elsie scoffed at him. "Nee, no better than the others, I'm sure," she said modestly. "Besides, I think she had a hope that one of my older brothers would escort her home from a singing."

At that comment, they both laughed.

It felt good to laugh. Elsie realized that it had been a long time she had thought about such things as the past. School? Friends? Teachers? "I wonder whatever happened to that Linda Zook from Ohio," she said softly.

His eyes softened. "Most likely passed on by now," he admitted. "She was a gut eight years older than us...maybe ten."

They fell silent again. Death. It always came back to that. At 75 years of age, it was impossible to avoid it. Death surrounded the elderly and, if they were lucky, it would be someone else's.

Elsie took a deep breath and, with the slightest of hesitations, leaned forward. "I have a question for you, Bishop," she began. She was glad that he didn't correct the use of his title rather this given name. "I've been giving a lot of thought to this."

"What is it, Elsie?"

"Well," she started, running her wrinkled finger along the rim of her mug. "The Bible says that we won't know each other in heaven, ain't so? Yet, the Bible says that we will be happy in heaven. We will experience joy." She paused and stared at the tea. She needed to know the answer but she was afraid the bishop would be upset that she was questioning both him and the Bible. "Ach vell," she continued, the nervousness apparent in her voice. "It saddens me to think that when I go to heaven I won't know Bruder Stephen or Mamm or Daed. Without knowing them, I don't think I could experience joy in heaven." She looked up, her eyes meeting Jacob's in the shadows that were cast around the room from the kerosene lantern. "Do you think I will know him, Bishop?"

His reaction startled her for he had no reaction. Not at first anyway. He held her gaze as he contemplated the question. It was not a typical question that he was asked. He was used to questions about the sins of the world such as the rights and wrongs of using cellphones, solar panels, and fertilizer from the store. This, however, was a deeper question that required a more structured answer.

"Do you, Bishop?" she pressed him.

He cleared his throat. "I think you are asking that for a different reason, Elsie."

"Different?"

With a nod of his head, he repeated. "Ja, a different reason. The thought of eternity alone frightens all of us, ja? Mayhaps you are missing your bruder and thinking that eternity begins now."

Elsie felt stung by his words. For a moment, she wanted to lash out and argue with him, deny what he said to her. However, arguing wasn't her way, nor was reacting in such a manner. Besides, she thought as she digested his words, there was a kernel of truth to his suggestion. Indeed, she was worried about being alone, the last of the family, living by herself and aging more rapidly than she had ever thought possible.

What if she fell down the basement stairs?

What if she lost her balance in the shower?

What if she had a stroke and there was no one to help her?

These were the questions that plagued her. If the idea of living in eternity alone, without knowing her own bruders and shweshters, her mamm and daed, frightened her, Jacob was correct that the idea of living in life alone frightened her just as much. Simply put, she didn't want to find herself suffering alone. One fall, one slip, one debilitating stroke and she would be suffering alone, in her own home, until someone thought to check on her.

"I miss my bruder," she admitted. "I miss taking care of him, this is true." She lifted her tired eyes to meet the bishop's.

"But what I miss the most is not being alone."

He nodded. "I understand."

She frowned. "Do you? You have a wife and you have kinner and you have little ones that visit. You are truly never alone, Jacob."

"That is true, too," he said slowly, his finger toying with the edge of the table. "But one can have all of those things and still feel alone, Elsie."

Alone? The bishop? He had married in his twenties, shared fifty years with the same woman. Elsie knew they had eight kinner and she reckoned they had almost seventy grand kinner with quite a few great-grandchildren in the mix. How could one feel alone with so many offspring and family to visit and keep him company? "I don't understand."

He glanced at her then looked away. There was a pained look in his expression and immediately she wondered what was bothering him. In all the years that she had known Jacob Beiler, he had always been so upbeat and positive, a quick smile for anyone and a willing ear for those in need. It was a curiosity to her that, tonight, his confidence and happiness both looked to be lacking.

"I suppose I shouldn't be talking about this," he said slowly, still avoiding her eyes. "I've had a good life, you see."

"I know you have, Jacob," she said softly.

"My Mary is a godly wife, a wonderful mother, and a right gut friend," he said firmly. "It's been fifty years, Elsie. That's a long time." He looked up and met her gaze. "But I always wonder one question..." His voice trailed away.

A question? What question could he possibly have to ask? Every man prayed for what Jacob Beiler had. A wife who followed God and the Ordnung as if they were one and the same. A woman who raised eight children, all of whom took the kneeling vow and joined the Amish church. And a friend to travel life alongside him, a companion to praise his achievements and console him in the face of failure. No, Elsie thought. There could be no "what if" when it came to Mary Beiler.

"What is that question, Jacob?" she asked, mostly because she suspected he wanted her to probe deeper.

With a deep breath, he leaned back in the chair and stared at her. The chair creaked under his weight. He wasn't a young, handsome twenty year old anymore, that was for certain. But, as he gazed at her, she didn't see a man in his seventies. "What if it had been you who took that lemonade from me at the singing and not Mary," he responded, his eyes troubled and worried as the words slipped past his lips.

For a long moment, she wasn't certain how to respond. Instead, her mind tripped back in time, stumbling over years of memories as she sought the dusty corner of her brain for a hidden door, one that she had kept locked for oh so long! Blowing the cobwebs off that key, she fit it into the lock, turned it, and watched with baited breath as the door opened...

She was eighteen and sitting on a hay bale with her friends. It was a Sunday evening at the Miller's farm, an evening set aside for the youth to gather in order to sing, socialize, and relax. Elsie was laughing with Anna and Mary about the kitten that had wandered into the church service earlier that day.

Church had been held at the Miller's farm in the barn. Being that it was summer, it was too hot to have service in the house. Instead, the barn suited just perfect, especially with the doors open and a warm morning breeze blowing through the room.

Bishop Glick had been preaching, another long sermon about the evils of the world and how young folk were taking too much liberty with their rumschpringe by attending those fancy movie theatres in the bigger towns. The younger attendees were trying to not pay any attention to the movement behind the open doorway from the large gathering room above the main barn floor. However, the young ladies had the perfect vantage point to see the grey striped kitten saunter around the doorframe, rubbing its back against the woodwork. It stopped to lick its paw for a moment then, its head shot up, staring at the crowds of people seated on the hard, backless benches, as if noticing them for the first time.

Bishop Glick indicated that it was time to pray. Everyone stood up, faced the outer wall and, as if on silent command, dropped to their knees to press their heads against folded hands on the benches. Their eyes were supposed to be shut and Elsie was following orders until she heard a very strange news in the silence that engulfed her. Purring. And it was loud. Even more troubling, it was right by her side.

Elsie peeked open one eye and saw the kitten, a tiny and fuzzy grey striped kitten, rubbing its body against the back of someone's shoe. Whoever was kneeling before her tried to shoo the kitten away by wiggling her foot. This only incited the kitten more and she began swatting at the giant black shoe.

With every ounce of her might, Elsie held back her laughter at the sight of the woman and the kitten engaged in a silent battle during an even more silent prayer. Her sides began to ache as she held back her mirth at the situation. Squeezing her eyes shut, she tried to forget what she had just witnessed. If she laughed in church, Bishop Glick would be sure and certain to give her a private tongue lashing later.

Later that evening, at the youth gathering, Elsie shared the story with her friends. She was astonished to learn that they, too, had seen the kitten and had fought as hard as they could to not break into laughter. They broke into giggles, trying to imagine what would have happened if just one of them had broken the silence.

"You girls sure do seem to be having fun," a voice said from behind Elsie.

Anna and Mary smiled at whoever it was but Elsie had to crane her neck in order to see Jacob Beiler standing at her back. Tall and handsome Jacob Beiler with dark brown hair and big green eyes smiled when she recognized him. Elsie flushed at the attention he had afforded the group of girls and turned away.

That didn't stop Jacob from walking around the hay bales to stand before Elsie and the other girls. He was holding a cup of lemonade in his hand, a smile still plastered on his face. For a split second, Elsie wondered if he was nervous. He sure seemed to be acting that way, especially with the way he kept shifting his weight and staring at her.

"What are you laughing about, then?" he asked.

Elsie averted her eyes. Despite being of the age to court, she had not pursued anyone nor had she encouraged any of the boys to pursue her. For Elsie, she was waiting for someone special. Someone who gave her goose bumps when he stared at her with those emerald eyes and perfect smile.

It was Mary who answered. "Church today. Did you boys see the kitten on our side of the room?"

"Nee," he responded but his eyes were still on Elsie. "Glad the kitten was on your side. Surely would have caused a few giggles on ours."

Silence. It was as if the girls were waiting for Jacob Beiler to explain why he had joined them.

Finally, with a slight shuffle of his feet, Jacob cleared his throat and said, "Wanted to know if you'd like some fresh lemonade."

It appeared that he was reaching out the cup to hand it to her. Elsie's heart lurched into her throat. Had Jacob Beiler actually thought to bring her a lemonade? There was an odd flutter inside of her chest as she contemplated the meaning of such an action. If he did, that surely meant he wanted to take her home in his buggy after the singing!

But it was Mary who took the cup of lemonade and thanked Jacob Beiler. She was standing closest to him since Elsie was seated on the hay bale. It was clear that the lemonade had been intended for Elsie but her mind had been in such a whirl that she hadn't acted quickly enough. That had made Elsie's hesitation seem a bit too drawn out and, in order to save Jacob from a potentially embarrassing situation, Anna had accepted the lemonade and sealed everyone's fate.

It was the following week that one of her older bruder's wife was injured and Elsie had volunteered to help her bruder with the kinner. She wound up staying at Isaiah's farm for almost six weeks. By that time, Jacob and Anna had started courting and, by fall, their marriage had been announced. It was a rapid courtship but not unheard of in the Amish community.

So, when Elsie attended their wedding, she tried not to look at Jacob with the eyes of envy but of happiness that he had *found such a wunderbaar gut woman to share his life.*

Elsie blinked her eyes. The memory faded and she looked up at Jacob. For that moment, that briefest of seconds, she saw him as he was then, a young man with a good future ahead of him. She saw him as the one man that had interested her enough to dream until she hesitated too long to take that cup of lemonade then offered to help her bruder's family. It dawned on her that her entire life was the same story. Self-sacrifice that led to missed opportunity.

"I...I don't know what to say to that, Jacob," she whispered. Inside her chest, her heart ached. She forced other memories away. It was too painful to see it all at once.

"You are a right gut woman," Jacob said. "I knew that you had gone to help your bruder and I didn't wait." He paused, glancing at her before he quickly added, "I'm not complaining, Elsie. I've had a wunderbaar life."

She frowned. "Then why are you telling me this?"

He took a deep breath and stared at her. "Because I know the sacrifices you have made. I wanted you to know that you helped many people...in fact, you changed lives. Selflessness can do that and it often isn't repaid." He paused and averted his eyes. "I wish I could repay you for what you did for me. For the life I have with Mary."

A light flashed outside the door and Elsie looked up. A shadow passed before the window and the glasses rattled again as someone tapped on it. Another visitor?

The interruption ended the conversation. Bishop Beiler stood up and collected his hat. He stood back while Elsie hurried to the door and opened it.

"I saw your light on and a buggy in the driveway," a cheerful voice said. "Hope I'm not disturbing you, Elsie, but I wanted to bring you a platter for supper! And some company to pass away some time presently!"

Elsie stepped back and a tall, willowy woman stepped into the kitchen. She had a navy knit handkerchief tied over her head and a thick but dirty black coat covering her maroon color dress.

"Why Bishop!" the woman said, flashing a bright and sunny smile that lit up the room better than the kerosene lantern. "I didn't know you were here!"

"Rachel Ann," the bishop said with a stiff nod of his head. Gone was the casual Jacob Beiler with flashing green eyes. Instead, the stern bishop, the leader of the community, had returned and stood in her kitchen. It was as if the knock on the door had transformed him. "I was just getting ready to leave."

After saying a quick good-bye and wishing the ladies both a Merry Christmas, Jacob Beiler slide his black hat back onto his head and, with one last nod at Elsie, slipped out the door and hurried to his buggy.

Elsie shut the kitchen door but stood there, for just a moment, listening to Rachel Ann hurry about the kitchen. Instead of joining her, Elsie watched as the bishop backed his horse and buggy away from the post in her driveway. She saw him glance once at the house before he slapped the reins on the horse's back and drove the buggy out onto the road, disappearing into the darkness as if he had never been there at all.

Chapter Four

"Now Elsie," Rachel Ann said as she moved about the kitchen. "I thought that I'd bring you a Christmas present!" She laughed and motioned toward the food that she had set out upon the counter. "A feast, ain't so!"

Elsie frowned and stared at the different serving bowls: ham, mashed potatoes with gravy, pickled cabbage, baby carrots with maple syrup, red beets, and green bean salad. The bowls were steaming, obviously still warm from having been cooked next door. Despite having thought she would only reheat some soup, Elsie had to admit that it sure looked wunderbaar gut! She couldn't remember the last time she had seen such a feast in her own kitchen. Certainly not since Stephen passed, that was for sure and certain.

"Rachel Ann," Elsie started to protest, perhaps not as vehemently as she would normally do, "I've told you in the past to not worry about me."

With a distracted wave of her hand, Rachel Ann began to set the bowls on the table, hustling back and forth as she moved. She was comfortable in the kitchen, even thought it was not her own. "Nonsense," she scoffed. "It's not worry that brings me here, Elsie." Setting down two plates and utensils on the table, Rachel Ann looked up and motioned for Elsie to sit. "It's because we all love you so!"

"You shouldn't do this," Elsie responded, her words sounded feeble and meek, overwhelmed by emotion as she felt.

"We may not have a lot but what we have, we share with our family, friends, and dear neighbors," Rachel Ann said lightly. "Now, you sit yourself down while I get some nice, cool water. Then, let's eat and enjoy each other's company, shall we?"

We? That word took Elsie by surprise. After all Rachel Ann had her own family, a husband and five young kinner. She should be having Christmas Eve supper with them. But Elsie knew better than to argue with Rachel Ann. She might be young but she was known to be strong-willed when it came to caring for others.

After they bowed their head in a silent prayer, Rachel Ann began passing the plates. She put small helpings on her own plate but large, heaping portions on Elsie's.

"That's too much," Elsie protested. "I don't want to waste any. I don't have the same appetite I once did!"

Again, Rachel Ann dismissed her with a simple wave of her hand. "There's plenty and I know you don't eat right. I keep inviting you over but you keep refusing. So," she said as she passed a bowl of applesauce to Elsie. "If you won't come to me, I shall come to you." Looking up, Rachel Ann smiled, clearly pleased to be visiting with Elsie and not at all feeling inconvenienced.

"That's awful kind," Elsie said softly, humbled by this good woman's generosity.

"Saw your nephew here the other week," Rachel Ann said, watching as Elsie dished the applesauce into the small bowl next to her plate. "Menno's a right gut man," she said.

"Ja, that he is. Stops by each week to check on me," Elsie said humbly.

"You going to his house for supper then, tomorrow?"

Oh, he had asked her. A dozen times. But Elsie didn't

want to be a bother. They had all those kinner and dairy work. His wife, Melinda, was always busy baking bread or making cheese to sell in town. Like so many others, they struggled to make do, but they certainly didn't have enough for one more mouth. At least that was what Elsie constantly told Menno when he invited her to visit for an evening meal. His persistence was not as strong as her desire to not be a bother to anyone.

"Nee," Elsie said. "With all the work he has to do, too much bother to come get me, I told him."

At that, Rachel Ann frowned. "Now Elsie," she said, taking the applesauce back and dishing some in her own bowl. "You can't be like that. And you need to eat."

"I'm eating now, ain't so?"

Rachel Ann frowned. "You need a gut supper on Christmas, I reckon!" Pause. "But you also need a gut supper every night!"

"I eat," Elsie said feebly, knowing that it wasn't always exactly true. If Rachel Ann hadn't stopped by, Elsie never would have reheated that soup for supper. She would have gone to bed without having eaten a thing.

"And if you don't start eating right, I'm going to have to make you some new dresses! You've lost weight, Elsie," she fussed. "But look at this dress I have on. It's a new fabric from the dry goods store. So soft and warm. Here, touch the bottom!" Without waiting for her response, Rachel Ann lifted up the corner of her dress and thrust it into Elsie's hand. "Isn't it just divine? Mayhaps I'll make you a dress anyway. You'd like right smart in a new maroon dress from this fabric."

She continued to talk, filling the room with a joyful

noise of happiness and stories from her life that Elsie found herself staring at this amazing young woman. Rachel Ann had always been a jovial person, quick to smile and laugh. Other women called her easy-going, kind, and big hearted. Elsie was blessed to also call her a neighbor.

Was it already eleven years since Rachel Ann had moved into the farmette next door? They had been young and just married but less than six months. It was only four acres and not large enough to sustain a living through farming. So her husband, John David, hired himself out as a landscaper, doing what he could to drum up business from the Englischers that lived nearby. There were always plenty of people who were too busy for yard work. The only problem was that John David didn't drive. It was hard to travel too far and he certainly couldn't bring lots of equipment.

It was happening to more and more families. The larger farms passed down from generation to generation. Still, with many Amish families having eight to ten children, that left a great need for homes since farms were in short order.

The overflow was noticeable by all. Some of the towns located just outside of Lancaster were overcrowded. Major roads were clogged with traffic, especially during the summer when tourist season was at its peak. Developments were springing up overnight on what used to be rich farmland. Some families were moving west. Missouri and Montana were increasingly popular. The others tried to make due with newer houses on smaller properties. They would have enough property for a horse and a few cows and chickens. They could certainly have a nice sized family garden. But that was about it.

Still, it wasn't the housing that was a problem. It was work. Indeed, without farming and with limited positions in

Amish stores, there simply weren't many options. Despite their best efforts to avoid the worldliness of the non-Amish, finding work among the Englische was often the only solution.

In the case of Rachel Ann, Elsie knew that the family fell into the category of one that was struggling financially. Rachel Ann worked from before sunrise to well into the night, making cheese and jams to sell at the roadside stand where their eldest daughter, Mabel, worked during the summer and after school. She was only ten years old but her long hours, standing in the dilapidated road side food stand, added considerable income to the family.

"My Mabel made that applesauce this fall past," Rachel Ann said proudly. "Made 200 quarts for sale and another 100 quarts for our own pantry!"

"She's a gut girl," Elsie said, and she meant it.

"She's out with her youth group right now," Rachel Ann said, her voice happy and cheerful. "She and John Junior. Running with the school group to sing Christmas carols at the older people's homes." For a moment, Rachel Ann flushed. They both silently wondered if the group of children would stop at Elsie's to sing a tune or two.

It was a custom among the Amish for the school aged children to visit those that were older or widowed or infirmed. They would sing carols as a way of warming the homes of those who were quite often lonely during the winter months, especially during the holiday season.

Elsie always kept crocheted bookmarks and doilies handy in case the children came by. She remembered the last Christmas when Stephen was still with her. The children had sung such a beautiful iteration of Shepherds! Shake Off Your

Drowsy Sleep. She could still hear their sweet, innocent voices as they sang her favorite verse:

> Hark! Even now the bells ring round,
> Listen to their merry sound;
> Hark! How the birds new songs are making,
> As if winter's chains were breaking.

Hearing the children had lifted Stephen's spirits, despite the fact that he was ailing even back then.

"I know it's cold out but I bundled those two children right gut and sent them with warm potatoes in their pockets!" She laughed as if the thought amused her. "John Junior was horrified at the thought, walking around with a steaming potato in his pocket but that Mabel told him that he'd sure be appreciative later on! Can't wait to hear about it."

"And your John David? Where is he that you can spend supper with me?" Elsie asked slowly, with a touch of guilt in her voice. She felt guilty knowing that Rachel Ann was not with her husband and her own family on Christmas Eve. She didn't want to come between a man and wife on such a special night. *After all,* she thought, *who am I to take Rachel Ann away from her family?*

It was as if Rachel Ann could read her thoughts. She set her fork down and reached over to cover Elsie's hand. With steady eyes, she stared at the older lady, a soft smile on her face. "Don't you worry about that John David. I made certain that he and the other kinner were just fine, Elsie. You always worry about everyone else. Mayhaps it's time to let others worry about you, ja? Stop fighting others' wish to care for you...at least just for once."

Elsie stared at Rachel Ann, speechless. The words that she had just spoken echoed in her brain. It hadn't been that long ago that someone else had said similar words, almost verbatim. Once again, she found herself floating in her memory to a time way back when...

It was her mamm. She wasn't doing well. Her breathing had slowed and she struggled to talk. She had been suffering for months while the cancer was spreading. During that time, Elsie had never left her side. She spent every waking moment with her mamm, even sleeping in a chair beside the bed at night so that her mamm never had to be alone.

During the day, Bruder Stephen would give Elsie some relief. He would sit with their mamm so that Elsie could hitch up the horse and buggy to run some errands in town. There was always the need to do food shopping at the Natural Food Store down Mulberry Lane. The quick errands were welcomed respites but she often found herself worrying the entire time, hoping that Stephen hadn't left Mamm's side. Other times, Elsie tended to some chores in the house: laundry needed washing, floors needed scrubbing. There was always something to do when Stephen offered to spend time with Mamm. Rarely, Elsie simply took a nap in the bedroom. She didn't realize it at the time but it had been well over two months since she had slept in her own bed at night.

Elsie never complained.

Instead, she knew that each day was a blessing from the Lord. She woke up and, after seeing that her mamm was still breathing, Elsie would fall to her knees and send her prayers of gratitude to God. One more day, she would pray each morning. That's all I had asked for in my prayers and, once again, you provided. I thank You, Lord.

Elsie would spend hours reading to her mamm from the Ausbund or daily devotionals. Mamm especially loved the sixteenth verse of Song 87 of the Ausbund:

So let us now love God,
However not with words alone,
But in truth and in deed,
Upon earth in all places,
Let us do good to His children
All Together,
God will have pleasure in this,
When we esteem His children.

Often, her mamm would wave her hand when she was finished, indicating that she wanted Elsie to repeat what she had just read.

"It's all about loving God through loving His children," her mamm would say with a raspy voice. "And you, dear Elsie, are one of His children, indeed."

Sometimes, the ladies from the church would come to visit on a Saturday morning. On these days, Elsie would hustle about the kitchen, eager to bring fresh meadow tea for refreshment on warmer days or quick to offer them fresh, homemade oatmeal cookies. The ladies would laugh good-naturedly, amazed with Elsie's insistence on serving them when it was their intention to give Elsie a break for an hour or so.

"No time for a break," she would explain softly. She didn't finish the sentence but they knew what she meant. After her mamm passed, she thought, then I can take a break.

"You're wearing yourself out, Elsie," her bruder complained. "You need to rest."

"Nee," she retorted without so much as a second thought.

"Mamm never rested when we were kinner, ain't so? She was always there for us. I need to be there for her now."

Stephen had merely frowned at her. "You are always there for everyone, Elsie."

And then came the day...

Her mamm was feverish but more coherent than in days past. Elsie was placing ice chips on her lips and talking with her, asking her mamm if she wanted a cool cloth on her head or if she needed to use the toilet. Her mamm reached out a weathered and tired hand, placing it on Elsie's arm. The gesture caused Elsie to stop talking and cease fussing over her mamm.

"Elsie," her mamm whispered.

"What is it, Mamm? More chips? Or, mayhaps, some applesauce?" She reached for the plastic cup of crushed ice that she had on the metal folding table by her mamm's bedside.

"Stop. You worry too much about everyone else," her mamm said, her voice thick and raspy. "When will there be time to worry about yourself, Dochder? Soon enough will that time come that you must let others care for you for a spell."

"Mamm?" Elsie asked, confused. Her mamm never spoke like that to her.

"Don't fight others caring for you anymore," her mamm whispered, the words barely audible.

Those were the last words that her mamm ever said to her. Not even an hour later, she fell into a sleep, a sleep that never ended and one that left Elsie stunned as she stared at the shell of woman that looked so peaceful in death. She was well into her 90s. Her death shouldn't have come as a surprise and certainly not as a shock. But Elsie felt an emptiness grow inside of her as she stared at her mamm. She didn't even call for

Stephen to tell him. She sat there, holding the now cold hand of her mamm, knowing that once she'd let go, she'd never feel it again.

"Elsie?"

Rachel Ann's voice startled her out of her remembrance. Snapping back to the present, she gazed at the young woman before her. She was so full of life and love, optimism and hope. Had Elsie ever had such joy in her life?

Indeed, she thought, probably not. When she was younger, she took care of the younger kinner. When she was older, she took care of her siblings' children. As she aged, she began to care for her older parents. Finally, it was Stephen's needs that she tended until, at last, there was no one left to care for. *No one,* she realized, *but myself.*

"I'm sorry," she said, shaking her head. "I must be getting ferhoodled in my old age."

Rachel Ann gave her an understanding smile. "It's getting late. You must be tired. I didn't mean to take up so much of your time, chatting about the going-ons at my house and about my kinner! But you let me just clean up these dishes, lickety split!"

"I can help," Elsie said meekly, still shaken by the memory of her mamm's last words.

"Of course you can," Rachel Ann said, stressing the word *can.* "But you let me take care of this. And I still want you to consider coming over tomorrow for Christmas supper. No gut being alone on Christmas."

There was that word again: alone. Elsie knew that the opposite of alone meant being with people, lots of people. And that meant she was infringing on other's quality time with their family. It wasn't their fault that she didn't have family left anymore, she thought with sorrow in her heart. Yet, for just a moment, she wondered what it would be like to accept such offers of kindness.

"That's not my fate," she whispered.

Rachel Ann looked up from the soapy water in the kitchen sink. "What's that, Elsie?"

Shaking her head, Elsie forced a meek smile. "Nothing, Rachel Ann. Just getting tired, tis all." As if on cue, the clock in the sitting room rang eight times.

"Goodness me!" Rachel Ann exclaimed as she glanced at the battery operated clock on the stove. "Look at the time! I didn't realize it was so late! You go on get yourself ready for bed, if that's what you want. I'll just let myself out, then."

That was the last thing Elsie wanted. Going to bed early meant she would wake up early. She'd be waking up alone for the first time on Christmas Day. There was nothing she dreaded more than that. Certainly there would be no visitors. Everyone would be busy sharing a warm Christmas breakfast with their own families, whether it was a simple fare of eggs and toast for those struggling to make ends meet or a more elaborate breakfast for those who were better established.

Chapter Five

It was the middle of the night when she woke up. The room was dark and quiet. She was alone.

Or was she?

For a long time, she laid in bed and listened to the quiet. No noise. No movement. Nothing.

Then, she heard it. The gentle tick, tock, tick tock of the clock in the sitting room. At first, it was soft, barely audible. But as the quiet faded away, the noise grew louder until she felt as if she was in the same room with the clock. Clearly, she thought, there is no more sleep for me this evening.

Pushing back the quilt, she sat up and eased her legs over the side of the bed. The air in the room was surprisingly warm, not cold as it normally would be in the middle of a December night. She purposefully kept the house cold at night as she found that she slept better that way. But not tonight. Tonight, as she has predicted, she had gone to bed too early and now she was wide awake, in the dark, on an early Christmas morning...and alone.

"Oh help," she muttered to herself.

Elsie? Elsie? Can you get up? Can you hear me?

She blinked in the darkness. Where did that memory come from? That voice?

Call for help.

She shut her eyes and concentrated. She searched the depths of her memory. Had she ever needed anyone to call for help? Oh, she had been sick in her day. A cold here, a flu every few years. But she had never needed "help." Where was this memory hiding in her past? She frowned and tried to dust the cobwebs from her brain. But nothing came to mind.

I just found her here. She was alone.

It was a male voice. A young male voice, at that. Familiar but yet, she couldn't place it. At least not at first.

We had told her to let us take care of her, the voice said.

Now that voice was recognizable, even despite the grief: It was Menno's.

"Stop!" Elsie exclaimed out loud, a bead of sweat suddenly appearing on her forehead. She felt hot, wishing for a moment that she could step outside and let the coldness of the Christmas Eve night wash over her, cooling her and erasing the memories that were so daunting and sad.

Quickly, she stood up and reached for her robe. Covering her shoulders, she hurried to light the lantern on her nightstand by dragging a match against the strike pad that she kept on the wall right by the door. The flame whispered as it cast a glow in the room, which only grew as she lifted the glass hurricane and lit the wick. Waving the match, she made certain it was out before she set it in the small glass bowl that she kept on her nightstand for just that purpose.

Alone?!

A different voice repeated that offending word. She suddenly realized how horrible that word sounded. *Alone.* It reverberated in her head. After all of these years, was that what she had to look forward to? Being alone? Being haunted by memories of the past and visions of the future? It was certainly not an appealing thought.

Elsie clenched her teeth and grabbed the lantern, hurrying out of the bedroom. The realization that senility was starting to set in frightened her. She hoped that leaving the bedroom would make it go away. What would happen to her, she wondered, if she told anyone that she was hearing voices talking about her at night?

In the kitchen, she put water in her dented silver kettle and placed it on the stove. Flipping the knob, she listened to the hissing noise of the flame emanating from the stovetop. It was a reassuring noise. Something she was used to. Anything to get the echoes of the word *alone* out of her head, she thought.

When had it gotten to this point? Why was she the last of the family and the one to face a future of loneliness on her own? Everyone else had passed away, gone to meet the heavenly Father, while she was left behind to wake up to an empty house and a deep silence that was only broken by the whisper of words in her head.

She stood at the back kitchen window, staring out at the farmer's field behind her house. In the moonlight, it looked silvery blue with shadows casting over the empty fields. On the horizon, just barely, she could make out the outer buildings, the dairy barn and the horse stables. The house was smaller and completely dark except for one light, a simple glow from an upstairs window, a glow that seemed to grow brighter as she was watching it.

It must have been her imagination, she reckoned.

Yet she continued to watch it. Mayhaps because it was an inviting light, a glow that suddenly seemed to blaze. It filled her with a warmth that spread throughout her chest. *God's light*, she thought. In that instant, she understood it all and knew what the past twelve hours had all truly meant.

For the first time in a long time, she felt at peace.

You understand now?

The voice was inside of her head but she wasn't afraid anymore. It was Stephen and Jacob and Rachel Ann all wrapped into one tone. It was the past, the present, and the future staring at her and telling her something very important, something that only she could act upon in order to change the final years of her life.

She nodded her head, although no one was around to see her. *Yes,* she thought. *I understand it all.*

Chapter Six

Elsie wasn't surprised when she heard the buggy pull into her driveway at precisely seven in the morning. In fact, she was prepared. She had dressed in a clean blue dress with long sleeves and a freshly ironed black apron, waiting. If she was asked how she knew that Menno would show up, she wouldn't have been able to answer the question. But she had known to expect her youngest nephew and she knew what was about to transpire.

The knock at the door was soft, as if afraid to startle her. But Elsie was on her feet and pulling at the doorknob within seconds of the noise. Flinging the door open, she greeted Menno with a warm smile and a friendly, "Merry Christmas, Menno!"

If he had been concerned that he would startle his elderly aunt, it was Menno who was surprised.

"Aendi," he said. "You are expecting someone?"

She laughed lightly. "I believe 'Merry Christmas' is the proper greeting on this wunderbaar gut day!"

He frowned at her. "Are you feeling alright, then?"

"Never better," she responded and took a step back. She gestured him inside. "It's cold. How about some tea or coffee to warm you, Menno?"

"Well," he started, slowly shutting the kitchen door behind himself. "That would be right nice, Aendi." He took off his gloves and shoved them into his coat pocket before he slid the coat off and hung it on the peg by the door. "Wanted to stop by and see how you were today. Wasn't certain if you were going anywhere for the day. If not...well, sure you won't say yes, you never do...but..." He paused. "Sure would be nice to have you come over and spend the day with my Melinda and the kinner."

She didn't respond right away. Her heart was racing and she quickly thought back to the events from the previous evening and early morning. Hustling in the kitchen, she poured him a steaming cup of coffee and put the cup on a tray with a bowl of sugar and creamer of milk before she carried it to the table. As she set it before him, she smiled but said nothing.

"Did you hear me, Elsie? Melinda and I just can't have you sitting here alone. Won't make our day happy," he said, reaching for the coffee cup. "I don't want to argue with you about it but..."

"Ja," she said softly.

"...no use being here alone," he continued as if he hadn't heard her. "You need to let others take care of you from time to..." He stopped. "What did you say?"

"I said 'ja'. I'll come."

Silence.

He hadn't expected that, hadn't thought that she would acquiesce without an argument or some sort of coercion. Her willingness stunned him into silence.

She smiled again, a soft and knowing smile. "You drink that coffee while I gather my things."

The ride in the buggy took just twenty minutes. Elsie was thankful that Menno had the forethought to bring some blankets. The air was crisp and cold, the kind of biting cold that could hurt Elsie, should she breathe it in through her nose. Instead, she lifted the edge of the blanket to cover her face and warm the air that she breathed.

The sky was grey. It hadn't snowed much this winter so far. Just a dusting that had remained sprinkled on the trees, especially the evergreens. Today, however, she could taste it in the air: a major snowfall was on its way. The day would soon find inches, perhaps even a foot, of snow on the ground. Of that, she was sure and certain.

She tried to think back to her own youth and snowy winter days. Snow meant sleigh riding down the hill behind the neighbors' barn. Elsie could still remember her older brothers, including Menno's father, John, helping her drag the sleigh up the hill when she was a young girl. It was an old sleigh with rusty runners. Her daed would use steel wool to rub the rust off and coat the runners with new paint. It didn't help. Each year, the runners would get rusty again. But Elsie didn't care.

The kitchen was ablaze in warm light from the kerosene lamps when Elsie walked inside. The air smelled like freshly baked bread and scrambled eggs. Melinda was at the counter, her back toward the door that Menno had just opened for his aunt.

"Back so soon, Menno?"

"Ja," he said. "And with a surprise!"

Melinda turned around and, when her eyes set on Elsie, she gave a broad smile and hurried over to greet her aunt with a warm hug. "Oh Elsie! What a gut surprise! I didn't think Menno would be able to convince you!" She looked back and forth from Elsie to her husband. "I'm so happy!"

"I didn't even need to convince her," Menno said, taking off his coat and hat. "It was as if she was expecting me!"

Melinda laughed and clapped her hands. "You were

expecting him, then?" She had always been a happy woman with a warm heart. But the joy in her voice was something that Elsie hadn't noticed before this moment. It was so sincere! Was she truly that overjoyed that Elsie was there for Christmas supper?

"I may have been," she responded. Then, handing Menno her black cape and bonnet, she looked around the kitchen. "The kinner are still sleeping?"

"Nee, nee," Melinda said, turning back to the counter. She had been making stuffing for a large turkey. From the looks of it, Elsie guessed it to be about twenty-five pounds. Melinda began spooning the stuffing into the cavity of the bird then, giving up, began to use her hands. "They are out milking the cows."

"All of them?" Elsie asked as she looked around.

Melinda laughed. "Yes, all the kinner except for the baby and Priscilla. They are still sleeping."

"Timothy?" Elsie asked, not believing what she was hearing. She couldn't remember the last time that she had seen Timothy. But she did recall that he had been barely able to walk on crutches.

"He's moving around right gut," Menno reassured her. "You would hardly know of the handicap."

"Oh, help!" Elsie said and clucked her tongue three times.

Menno laughed at Elsie's expression and walked over to Melinda. Placing his hand on her shoulder, he peered over to watch what she was doing. "That sure is one big bird for a not so big family," he teased.

Playfully, she nudged him with her arm. "You know that

my sister and her family are coming over."

Alarmed, Elsie started to say something, to protest that she would be too much extra trouble. Yet, as soon as that thought crossed her mind, she forced her mouth to stay shut. *No more*, she told herself. *No more.* So, instead, she took a deep breath and offered her assistance. "What can I do to help now, Melinda?"

The next hour passed quickly. Elsie helped clean the dishes from breakfast, washing and drying them before stacking them in the cabinet. She wasn't certain if Melinda had a fancy set of dishes for special celebrations such as Christmas or Easter. Instead of asking, she decided to wait to take direction from Melinda. For once, she would let someone else take charge and tell her what to do.

"Mamm! Mamm!" a voice called out from the washroom behind the kitchen. "It's snowing!"

Both Melinda and Elsie looked up, first glancing at the window and then toward the back door. In a flurry of activity, the young children tumbled into the room, their faces flushed pink from the outdoors and their eyes glowing.

"Aendi!" the youngest one cried out and ran to give her a big hug. "You came! You came!"

The warmth of the little arms around her waist touched Elsie. She shut her eyes and let herself enjoy it, if for just a moment. When was the last time a little one had hugged her? At Stephen's funeral? But this hug was so different. A hug of joy, not of sorrow. "Merry Christmas, Anna," Elsie said. "You smell like snow!"

Anna laughed, her brown eyes sparkling. "Snow doesn't smell, Aendi!"

"Don't sass your aendi," Melinda reprimanded gently. "And snow does smell. It smells fresh and cold...just like you!"

The other children began to giggle at the thought.

"Elsie! Will you show me how to crochet some bookmarks today?" It was Linda, the eight year old who asked that question. She was always begging to crochet new things. Bookmarks were the easiest to make, so Elsie was surprised that she would ask.

"Mayhaps another day," Elsie said. "It is Christmas, after all. No crocheting on such a day when we should be enjoying each other's company and thinking about baby Jesus."

Linda's smile disappeared.

Melinda tried to hide her own smile at her dochder's reaction. "Mayhaps a little wouldn't hurt, ja? After all, if you are doing it together, it's gut time spent together."

The kinner took off their coats and hung them on the pegs. Small puddles of melted snow dotted the floor. Without being asked, Linda took a rag from the bucket behind the door and wiped up the water so that no one would slip. In the meanwhile, the other kinner hurried upstairs to tidy their rooms and change out of their work clothes.

Elsie leaned against the counter and watched the energy of the young children as they dashed up the stairs. Their presence had energized the room, filling it with goodness and light that she hadn't felt in a long time. *I made the right decision,* she told herself.

"Aendi!" another voice called from the doorway.

When she turned around, she caught sight of young Timothy. He was at the door, a crutch under his arm and a smile on his face. He was taller than she remembered him and, when he crossed the room, he barely limped at all. Like a proper young man, he reached out his hand to greet his aunt with a warm handshake.

"Daed said you were here! We could barely wait to finish the barn chores!" His smile lit up her heart. A beautiful boy with a face like an angel, she thought "I hope we can play Scrabble later. Haven't played that with you in over a year, ain't so?"

She felt a lump in her throat. It had been the week before his accident but she didn't want to remind him of that. Melinda had brought the children over to her house to visit and Timothy had insisted that they'd play. He loved words and spelling them out on the Scrabble board. She had tried to play fairly but had won, nonetheless. It wasn't hard since he had been only seven at the time. But he wanted to show off his knowledge of spelling with his great-aunt.

"I'm much better now," he said proudly.

"Timothy," his mamm warned. "A haughty spirit goeth before a fall, ja?"

He lowered his eyes. "Sorry, Mamm," he said but peeked at Elsie. "But it's true," he whispered so that his mamm couldn't hear.

For the rest of the morning, the kitchen was a blur of activity and voices and laughter. Once the baby woke up, there was even more noise and even some crying. But it was all happy noises, a house full of love and life. Elsie sat in the rocking chair, holding the baby and just watched, observing all that was around her. The voices from the night before echoed in her head, dissipating amidst the activity that countered the one horrible word that continued to haunt her: *alone*. Nee, she thought. I'm not alone now.

It was during the Christmas supper that Elsie finally took a deep breath and looked up from her seat. She surveyed the faces of the adults and kinner that surrounded her. Melinda's sister and husband were chatting with Menno and Melinda about a neighbor while the children were helping themselves to a second round of mashed potatoes, cole slaw, and turkey.

Clearing her throat, Elsie caught Menno's attention. "I have an announcement," she said softly. "I want you all to hear it."

The room became silent as all eyes fell on the normally quiet Elsie. She took her time, looking at each and every one of them. Their eyes were bright and curious but also full of love.

"I have decided that I am going to move into your daed's old house," she said firmly, not wasting any time to get to the point. "I will live alone no more. I want to be around my family and share in your life."

Melinda gasped. "Oh Elsie!"

Menno frowned for a second then, as the words sunk in, he gave a broad smile. "That is right gut, Elsie! Right gut, indeed!"

The children clamored, the smaller ones bouncing in their seats although they weren't exactly certain what the announcement meant. Young Timothy reached out his hand and touched Elsie's arm. When she looked at him, he grinned. "We can play Scrabble all the time, then!"

"I hope you learned more words since we last played," Elsie teased lightly.

Menno nodded his head. "I couldn't have asked for a

better Christmas gift, Elsie. That grossdaadihaus has been empty for far too long. It will be gut for Melinda and for the kinner to have you stay here with us," he said. "And gut for you, too."

"Ja," she acquiesced. "Right gut for me, indeed! I don't want to be alone anymore." For a moment, she thought back to the voices that had taunted her last night. She didn't want that awful vision of the future to come to fruition.

Menno clapped his hands. "I think this calls for a family celebration!" He glanced around the room and smiled at the kinner. "Shall you kinner all sing a carol together to celebrate?"

Linda and Anna were the first to stand. The rest of the kinner followed their example and, within a short minute, they stood before the adults, smallest children up in front and the older ones in the back.

> *There's a gladness all around*
> *Christmas joy,*
> *There's a gladness all around*
> *Christmas joy.*
> *Smiles can easily be found*
> *Mirth and happiness abound,*
> *Christmas joy, Christmas joy*
> *Christmas joy, joy, joy.*

When the song was finished, Elsie smiled and wiped at the corner of her eyes. Indeed, she thought, there was joy in her heart today, a joy that would transcend Christmas. They continued to sing, moving onto the Angel's Song. Even Elsie had to join the chorus as the spirit lifted her spirit to share in the beauty of singing praise to the Lord and His son, Jesus:

> *Unto you is born this day*

Jesus to be King o'er all
Ye shall find Him on the hay
In a manger of a stall.

In Heaven glory,
In Heaven glory,
In Heaven glory,
And peace, good will on earth.

She felt the blessing of God bestowed upon her as she looked at the shining faces before her.

And, at this instant, Elsie realized that she had been given the greatest Christmas gift of all: The Gift of Love. A gift that all came about because of the visions of her past, present and future. From this moment onward, she would never feel lonely again.

Amish Carols

After having spent so many years among the Amish, it came as a complete surprise to me to learn that the Amish participate in singing Christmas carols. It was also a humbling experience because it taught me a valuable lesson: no matter how much you think you know about a culture and community, there are always surprises.

I was delighted to learn that the Amish children spend their "Christmas" days visiting the elderly, infirmed, and widowed to sing Christmas carols. I was also delighted to learn that they also present concerts at the school for the members of their community that wish to come visit and hear them sing Christmas carols.

I heard from my friends that the carols are sung in English, not Pennsylvania Dutch or German. I'm not certain if that is for all communities or just the one in which I have been accepted. One of the parents will hook up two mules (or horses) to a wagon filled with hay bales to drive the children from home to home. This usually happens during the week preceding Christmas in the afternoon when the children would normally be in school.

When I first heard this story, I was overcome with emotion. I stay with an elderly woman who has, basically, no siblings or immediate family left to tend to her needs. She takes care of herself. She has asked me, on more than one occasion, "Who will take care of me?" While I wish I could shout "Me! Me!", I know that is not the answer that she is seeking.

The answer, indeed, is God.

God will take care of her. Perhaps she forgets from time

to time but that is the truth that keeps her going. I remind her of the love that God has for her every time that I see her. More importantly, I see the love that the community has for this lovely woman. Her own nephew and neighbors tend to her needs on a daily basis, even when she doesn't need them.

My heartfelt wish for the rest of the world is to feel the love and the sense of community that is expressed in the world of the Amish. Many of you may never experience the world of the Amish firsthand but I am so blessed, and thankful, that I have been chosen to have the capability to share them with you. I often feel that we are missing something by not being Amish. So, to have the gift and passion to share it with my wonderful readers means more to me than you can imagine. I just want you to experience, even for a moment, the wonderful world that is known as the Amish.

The Amish Christian Class Series will continue. I hope you love reading them as much as I truly enjoy writing them.

Enjoy the stories. Enjoy the carols.

Christmas Joy

There's a gladness all around
Christmas joy,
There's a gladness all around
Christmas joy.
Smiles can easily be found
Mirth and happiness abound,
Christmas joy, Christmas joy
Christmas joy, joy, joy.

There's a bustle through the street
Christmas joy,
There's a bustle through the street
Christmas joy,
Bundles, bundles do we meet,
Laughing crowd and tripping feet,
Christmas joy, Christmas joy
Christmas joy, joy, joy.

There are some who do not know
Christmas joy,
There are some who do not know
Christmas joy,
To those poor brothers go,
And the seed of kindness sow,
Christmas joy, Christmas joy
Christmas joy, joy, joy.

Savory odors fill the air
Christmas joy,
Savory odors fill the air
Christmas joy,
Busy housewives everywhere
For a bounteous feast prepare,
Christmas joy, Christmas joy
Christmas joy, joy, joy.

Shepherds! Shake Off Your Drowsy Sleep

Shepherds, shake off your drowsy sleep,
Rise and leave your silly sheep.
Angels from heav'n around loud singing,
Tiding of great joy are bringing.

CHORUS
Shepherds! The chorus come and swell!
Sing Noel, O sing Noel!

Hark! Even now the bells ring round,
Listen to their merry sound;
Hark! How the birds new songs are making,
As if winter's chains were breaking.

See how the flow'rs all burst anew
Thinking snow is summer dew;
See how the stars afresh are glowing,
All their brightest beams bestowing.

Cometh at length the age of peace,
Strife and sorrow now shall cease;
Prophets foretold the wondrous story
Of this heav'n-born Prince of Glory.

Shepherds! Then up and quick away,
Seek the Babe ere break of day;

Prophets foretold the wondrous story
Of this heav'n-born Prince of Glory.

Shepherds! Then up and quick away,
Seek the Babe ere break of day;
He is the hope of ev'ry nation,
All in Him shall find salvation.

The Angels' Song

Sung to the tune: Jesus Loves Me

While the shepherds watch at night
On the hills near Bethlehem
Angels all in shining white
Singing, come from Heaven to them.

CHORUS
Come shining angels,
Come shining angels,
Come shining angels,
Come singing down to them.

Unto you is born this day
Jesus to be King o'er all
Ye shall find Him on the hay
In a manger of a stall.

CHORUS
In Heaven glory,
In Heaven glory,
In Heaven glory,
And peace, good will on earth.

About The Author

The Preiss family emigrated from Europe in 1705, settling in Pennsylvania as the area's first wave of Mennonite families. Sarah Price has always respected and honored her ancestors through exploration and research about her family's history and their religion. At nineteen, she befriended an Amish family and lived on their farm throughout the years. Twenty-five years later, Sarah Price splits her time between her home outside of New York City and an Amish farm in Lancaster County, PA where she retreats to reflect, write, and reconnect with her Amish friends and Mennonite family.

Contact the author at sarahprice.author@gmail.com.
Visit her weblog at http://sarahpriceauthor.wordpress.com or on Facebook at www.facebook.com/fansofsarahprice.

Made in the USA
Lexington, KY
22 October 2017